CENGAGE Learning

Poetry for Students, Volume 45

Project Editor: Sara Constantakis Rights Acquisition and Management: Margaret Chamberlain-Gaston Composition: Evi Abou-El-Seoud Manufacturing: Rhonda Dover

Imaging: John Watkins

Product Design: Pamela A. E. Galbreath, Jennifer Wahi Digital Content Production: Allie Semperger Product Manager: Meggin Condino © 2014 Gale, Cengage Learning

For product information and technology assistance, contact us at **Gale Customer Support, 1-800-877-4253.**

For permission to use material from this text or product, submit all requests online at **www.cengage.com/permissions**.

Further permissions questions can be emailed to **permissionrequest@cengage.com** While every effort has been made to ensure the reliability of the information presented in this publication, Gale, a part of Cengage Learning, does not guarantee the accuracy of the data contained herein. Gale accepts no payment for listing; and inclusion in the publication of any organization, agency, institution, publication, service, or individual does not imply endorsement of the editors or publisher. Errors brought to the attention of the publisher and verified to the satisfaction of the publisher will be corrected in future editions.

Gale
27500 Drake Rd.
Farmington Hills, MI, 48331-3535

ISBN-13: 978-1-4144-9506-4
ISBN-10: 1-4144-9506-4
ISSN 1094-7019

This title is also available as an e-book.

ISBN-13: 978-1-4144-9279-7
ISBN-10: 1-4144-9279-0
Contact your Gale, a part of Cengage Learning sales representative for ordering information.

Printed in Mexico
1 2 3 4 5 6 7 18 17 16 15 14

Half-Hanged Mary

Margaret Atwood 1995

Introduction

"Half-hanged Mary" is a poem by Canadian poet and novelist Margaret Atwood. It was published in Atwood's poetry collection *Morning in the Burning House* in 1995. The poem is based on a real incident that took place in Hadley, Massachusetts, in 1684. The previous year, a local woman, Mary Webster, had been charged with being a witch. In June, she was tried in Boston and acquitted. Her neighbors, however, appear to have been unconvinced by the verdict, and about eighteen months later, Webster was again accused of witchcraft. Some of the men from Hadley hanged her from a tree, but she managed to survive the ordeal. When townspeople came in the morning to cut her down, she was still alive. (There are other versions of this incident in the historical records.) She lived another eleven years, until her death in 1696. Atwood believed that Webster was her ancestor, and she dedicated her 1985 novel *The Handmaid's Tale* to her. The poem "Half-hanged Mary" is a dramatic monologue in ten sections that correspond to specific times, from 7 p.m. when Mary was hanged, until 8 a.m. the following morning, with a concluding section about her life in the years following the hanging. The poem, which exhibits Atwood's typical wit, subtlety, and sharp images, shines a light on a dark period in American history when irrationalism and fear led to persecution of the innocent.

Author Biography

Poet, novelist, short-story writer, essayist, and literary critic Margaret Eleanor Atwood was born on November 18, 1939, in Ottawa, Canada. Her father, Carl Edmund Atwood, was a forest entomologist; her mother, Margaret Dorothy (Killam), was a graduate in home economics from the University of Toronto. Atwood spent her earliest years in Ottawa during the winters and the rest of the year in northern Quebec and Ontario. In 1946, her father took up a position as professor at the University of Toronto, and the family moved to Toronto. In 1957, Atwood became a student of English at Victoria College, University of Toronto. In 1961, after graduation, she studied English at Radcliffe College, Harvard University, and was awarded a master's degree in 1962. She then went on to doctoral studies at Harvard until 1963. The following year, she taught English literature at the University of British Columbia. Her first collection of poetry, *The Circle Game* (1966), won the Governor General's Award. Since then, Atwood has published poetry, novels, short stories, children's literature, and nonfiction and has taught in many Canadian and American universities, including the University of Alberta, York University in Toronto, and New York University. Her works have been translated into more than forty languages, including Farsi, Japanese, Turkish, Finnish, Korean, Icelandic, and Estonian.

Atwood's many volumes of poetry include *The Animals in That Country* (1968), *The Journals of Susanna Moodie* (1970), *You Are Happy* (1974), *Two-Headed Poems* (1978), and *Interlunar* (1984). *Morning in the Burned House* (1995) includes the poem "Half-hanged Mary." This collection was a cowinner of the Trillium Award. Atwood's most recent collection, as of 2013, is *The Door* (2007).

Her fourteen novels include *The Edible Woman* (1969); *Surfacing* (1972); *Lady Oracle* (1976); *Life before Man* (1979); *Bodily Harm* (1981); *Encounters with the Element Man* (1982); *Unearthing Suite* (1983); *The Handmaid's Tale* (1985), which was a best seller and won the Governor General's Award, the *Los Angeles Times* Award, and the Arthur C. Clarke science fiction award; *Cat's Eye* (1988); *The Robber Bride* (1993), which won the Canadian Authors Association Novel of the Year Award; *Alias Grace* (1996), which won the Giller Prize; *The Blind Assassin* (2000), which won the Booker Prize; and the trilogy *Oryx and Crake* (2003), *The Year of the Flood* (2009), and *MaddAddam* (2013).

Atwood's nine short-story collections include *Dancing Girls and Other Stories* (1976), *Bluebeard's Egg and Other Stories* (1986), and *Moral Disorder and Other Stories* (2006); her nonfiction includes *Survival: A Thematic Guide to Canadian Literature* (1972) and *Payback: Debt and the Shadow Side of Wealth* (2008).

Atwood has worked and traveled extensively in Europe, and she has received honorary degrees from many institutions, including Trent University, Smith College, and the University of Toronto. She was president of the Writers Union of Canada from 1982 to 1983, and president of PEN International's Anglo-Canadian branch from 1984 to 1985. As of 2013, she is vice president of PEN International.

Atwood married James Polk, a novelist, in 1967. They divorced in 1973. Atwood lives in Toronto with Canadian writer Graeme Gibson. They have a daughter, Jess, who was born in 1977.

Poem Summary

The text used for this summary is from *Morning in the Burned House*, Houghton Mifflin, 1995, pp. 58–69.

The poem is divided into ten sections. Each section is headed by an exact time during which Mary, the woman who is being hanged, expresses her thoughts and feelings. The first section begins at seven o'clock in the evening. Mary recalls the circumstances in which she was seized. Rumors were flying around the town about witchcraft. She was milking a cow in the barn around sunset. The second stanza suggests that she was caught by surprise. She had no idea that she would be targeted as a witch. In the third stanza, she explains why she was picked on and hanged. First, she lived on her own; she was not married. (This is unlike the historical Mary Webster, on whom the poem is based, who was married.) Her appearance also helps to account for what happened to her, she thinks. She worked outside and got sunburned; her clothes were, it seems, not of the highest quality; and she owned the poorly kept farm where she lived. She also had knowledge of folk remedies for common ailments. In addition, as the last stanza of this section explains, she was a woman, and that made her a convenient target when people talked about demonic possession.

Section two starts one hour later, at eight

o'clock. Mary describes how she was hanged. The men from the town grabbed a rope and she was hanged from a tree. Her hands were bound, and she was gagged. The men, thrilled by what they had done out of hatred, trudged back home. Mary thinks that they were projecting their own evil onto her.

Section three begins at nine o'clock. Mary relates how some women from the town come to stare at her. Mary looks down from her position high up and can see how fearful they are. In the second stanza she addresses two of the woman directly. It appears that they are both friends of hers. Mary cured the baby of one of the women from some unspecified ailment; she helped save the life of the other one, it seems, by performing an abortion on her.

Mary knows that the women lack the courage to bring her down from the tree. Were they to do so, they might be accused of being witches too. It is better not to bring attention to oneself in this kind of situation, Mary says in the fourth stanza of this section. She understands that the women are unable to help her in any way at all.

At ten o'clock, which is the title of the next section, Mary addresses God directly. She wants to argue with him about free will. Was being hanged an act of free will on her part, a choice she made? She pours scorn on the concept of God's grace and suggests that the great Christian virtues of faith, hope, and charity are dead.

The next section begins at midnight. Mary

describes the unpleasant physical sensations she is experiencing. She is being strangled; she clenches her teeth; she feels despair. She feels the approach of death, personifying it first as a bird of prey, then as a venomous judge pronouncing punishment, and then as an angel urging her to give in to death.

By two o'clock in the morning, when the next section begins, Mary hears herself uttering some kind of sound. It seems that it is both a struggle for air and a prayer, born of desperation, that she might survive, that mercy might be shown to her.

By three o'clock, the wind is raging and the birds are singing. Mary's strength is ebbing and it is hard for her to breathe. However, she affirms her innocence and is determined not to give up.

At six o'clock, the sun rises. Mary feels she has been up there a thousand years. She makes a sardonic joke about having grown taller (she means her body has been stretched by hanging).

At eight o'clock, the townspeople come to cut her down from the tree. She is still alive. She knows that, according to the law, they will not be allowed to hang her again for the same offense. She grins at them. She looks at them and scares them. They run away. Mary reflects that, if she was not a witch before, she has become one now.

In the final section of the poem, Mary discusses her life since the hanging. She says she goes around mumbling to herself, and the townspeople flee from her whenever they see her. She finds that she can now say anything she wants;

having been hanged once, she cannot be hanged again. She also speaks of herself as having undergone two deaths. She eats a strange diet and commits blasphemies, she says. God understands her, she says, although no one else can. It seems that she has access to some secret knowledge or wisdom as a result of her ordeal, and she expresses it in words that only she and God can understand.

Topics for Further Study

- Write a poem in the form of a dramatic monologue. Remember that a dramatic monologue features a first-person speaker who is not the poet offering his or her thoughts and feelings about a particular situation to one or more people who are not actually present and whose reactions can be guessed only by the speaker's words. The situation can be based on a real event or it can be fiction.

- Give a reading of "Half-hanged Mary" to your class, preceded by a two-minute introduction in which you discuss the poem's theme and structure. Have a classmate record your reading and upload it to YouTube.

- Watch *The Crucible*, the 1996 film based on Arthur Miller's 1953 play that was itself based on the Salem witch trials. Using Internet sources, write a review of the film in which you assess how accurately the film conveys not only the facts but the atmosphere of those times. How does the film fictionalize the events, and in what respects does it stay close to the facts? Post your review to the Amazon website.

- Read *Where to Park Your Broomstick: A Teen's Guide to Witchcraft* by Lauren Manoy and Yan Apostolides (2002), which explains the principles of Wicca. It also includes a history of paganism and witchcraft. Write an essay in which you outline the basic elements of Wicca and describe how they resemble or differ from those of Christianity, Judaism, or any other major world religion. Comment also on the fact that the authors make no mention of the persecution of witches in history, including the witch hunts that took place in seventeenth-century New England. What reasons might the authors have had for omitting this? What is the relationship between the traditional understanding of witchcraft and the modern version found in Wicca?

Injustice

The speaker of the poem has suffered an injustice for which she was unprepared. The attack took her by surprise, and there has been no judicial process. The hanging she describes is an extrajudicial lynching. There is no evidence against her. Rumors have been flying around the town, she says in the first line of the poem, presumably about some unspecified act of so-called witchcraft, and Mary happens to be a convenient target for people who are looking for someone on whom to vent their anger and fear. Mary has done nothing to deserve it. In the section headed three o'clock in the morning, she affirms that she is innocent; she has committed no crime.

In the third stanza of the first section of the poem, Mary offers her own thoughts about why she was singled out. She was female, for a start, which made her more likely to be a target for the witch-hunters. She also lived alone and owned her own property. A woman owning property was not common in seventeenth-century New England and could have aroused resentment among men who felt it undermined their authority. The woman also practiced folk remedies; she says in this stanza that she knew a cure for warts. If someone in the town disliked her for some reason, the fact that she gave out remedies for common ailments and treated children (as she states in section three) might have been used against her if someone who took the remedy did not get better or even got worse. Such a situation might have led to an accusation that the woman had made a compact with the devil to do people harm. That such an accusation might have been made against the Mary of the poem is clear from the last stanza of the first section.

The injustice the speaker has suffered is also a betrayal, as the third section reveals. At least two of the women who come to look at her as she hangs from a tree were her friends. But the women will not help her, and Mary realizes that they are too fearful to do so. In this kind of situation, when irrational thinking has taken hold, it is dangerous to speak out against a prevailing view. The hatred unleashed against one person could, in a flash, turn against another.

Mary continues the theme of injustice is continued by Mary as she addresses God in the fourth section. God's love is absent from the universe that Mary inhabits as she hangs from the tree, and God offers her no assistance, nor any response at all. In the absence of God's grace, all that remains is the human idea of justice, which in this case is based on irrational fear and hatred.

Transformation

In this extremely unusual, macabre experience, Mary undergoes not death, as everyone including herself might have expected, but transformation. Her survival may, in part, be due to her mental strength. She refuses to give up, even though she is tempted to do so at midnight (tempted, it would seem, by the same devil that she is, supposedly, as a witch, in league with). At three o'clock in the morning, she remains defiant, still with the will to live. The first signs of her transformation are apparent at eight o'clock in the morning, when the men come to cut her down. The fact that she is still alive and grins at the men terrifies them, and they run away. Now she really is a witch, she says, with some wit, at the end of that section.

The final section of the poem describes Mary's life after her hanging. Marked out by her unusual, perhaps even unique, experience, she speaks of having died once already. She becomes an eccentric figure, talking strangely to herself, eating berries and flowers from the fields, and experiencing a freedom to do and say exactly what she wants, not fearing any reprisals. The townspeople are scared of her. It is as if she has acquired some kind of secret knowledge that enables her to communicate with nature. She seems to live a paradox: while being close to the earth, she is somehow also in touch with the divine. She has acquired a new language for understanding the mysteries of life that take her beyond the normal range of human knowledge. Although she now calls herself, with some irony, a witch, her communication is not with the devil but, in a sense, with God.

Style

Dramatic Monologue

The poem is in the form of a dramatic monologue. The dramatic monologue was made famous by the nineteenth-century English poet Robert Browning in poems such as "My Last Duchess" and "Andrea del Sarto." According to M. H. Abrams in *A Glossary of Literary Terms*, the dramatic monologue, as exemplified by Browning, usually consists of three elements. First, it features a single, first-person speaker who is not the poet, who gives his or her account of a specific event in which he or she is involved at an important moment during that event. Second, the speaker of the poem addresses one or more people in the course of the poem. Their responses are not given directly but can be inferred from what the speaker says. Third, the speaker, in explaining the situation, reveals his or her character.

The dramatic monologue has been used by many poets, including Alfred, Lord Tennyson, in "Ulysses," and T. S. Eliot, in "The Love Song of J. Alfred Prufrock." Atwood herself uses the form, with some variation, in "The Loneliness of the Military Historian," one of the poems in *Morning in the Burning House*. "Half-hanged Mary" meets all three elements identified by Abrams, with some variations. Mary, the speaker, is not the poet, and she relates a traumatic event that happened to her, extending the account to cover her life after the hanging. In addition to the reader, she addresses the women who come to stare at her in the evening (third section) and God (fourth section and part of the sixth section). She also shows herself to be a very spirited woman who possesses a sardonic sense of humor, as seen when she mocks her assailants and offers wry and witty observations about her own situation. She also reveals herself as a woman of great endurance and determination who is able to be defiant in the face of injustice and adversity to the extent that she is able to keep the flame of life alive within her.

Simile and Metaphor

The poem offers plentiful examples of simile and metaphor. Similes consist of a comparison between two unlike things in a way that brings out their underlying similarity. Similes are often recognizable by the words "as" or "like," and in this poem, the word "like" appears in this context no fewer than thirteen times. Each occurrence indicates the presence of a simile. For example, the accusation against her is compared to a bullet from a gun penetrating her. She compares herself as she is hoisted up onto the tree to a fallen apple being put back on the tree. In the section headed "midnight", the poet uses three similes, one after the other, for death. It is like a bird of prey, a prurient judge, or a persuasive, tempting angel. The poet even jokes about a simile that is not one. In the six o'clock section, the poet plays on the idea of the sun as a simile for God, which would be a common, scarcely original comparison, but the speaker gives it a twist: the sun is *not* a simile for God. Although it might have been in the past, the speaker implies, such a simile would no longer be appropriate for someone in her situation who is clinging to life in a universe in which God appears to be absent.

A metaphor occurs when two unlike things are linked not by a comparison between them but by identifying one as the other. In the eight o'clock section, Mary metaphorically becomes a flag, raised in the night. At the end of that section, the sky is a metaphor for the God who will not offer any solace or explanation for her fate.

Witches in Seventeenth-Century New England

Belief in witches was almost universal in the Puritan colonies of seventeenth-century New England. In a prescientific world, people believed in many things that modern people do not. Supernatural forces were thought to be at work in the day-to-day world, for example, and witches knew how to manipulate those forces for evil purposes. Witches, it was believed, had entered into a compact with the devil and were dedicated to inflicting harm on other people. If people were faced with a distressing event, such as illness, the death of a child, or the death of cattle, they might think that some evil force was at work and blame one of their neighbors whom they did not like or with whom they had recently quarreled or who was considered odd in some way.

David D. Hall, in his introduction to *Witch-Hunting in Seventeenth-Century New England: A Documentary History, 1638–1692*, notes that women, especially those over forty, were accused of being witches far more frequently than men were. The ratio was four to one. Men accused of witchcraft were also less likely to face trial, and their punishments were lighter than those meted out to women. Hall suggests that one reason for the discrepancy might have been because men held authority over women in all aspects of life and society. Witch-hunting might be seen as "a means of reaffirming this authority at a time when some women … were testing these constraints, and when others were experiencing a degree of independence, as when women without husbands or male siblings inherited property."

Legally, in New England in the seventeenth century, witchcraft was a felony punishable by death. The Puritans had scripture on their side in this respect, since the book of Exodus contains the statement, "Thou shalt not suffer a witch to live" (Exodus 22:18). The death penalty was carried out by hanging. Many alleged witches, however, were acquitted in trials, and people who made false charges against an alleged witch were subject to punishment themselves.

According to John Putnam Davos, in his introduction to *Entertaining Satan: Witchcraft and the Culture of Early New England*, throughout the seventeenth century in New England, there were a total of 234 cases in which indictments were made or complaints filed against accused witches. There were thirty-six executions. Twenty of these took place as a result of the notorious witch trials in Salem, Massachusetts, in 1692—just eight years after Mary Webster was hanged a little more than one hundred miles away in Hadley.

The Case of Mary Webster

Mary Webster lived in Hadley, Massachusetts. She married William Webster in 1670. They were poor and depended on the town for assistance. She was accused of witchcraft by the county magistrates in Northampton in March 1683. It appears that there were many written testimonies against her, naming her as a witch. The county magistrates sent her to Boston for further examination at the Court of Assistants. The court ordered her to stand trial, accusing her, as quoted in David Hall's *Witch-Hunting in Seventeenth-Century New England: A Documentary History, 1638–1692*, of having "familiarity" with the devil in the "shape of a warraeage [an Indian word meaning "black cat"] and had her imps sucking her and teats or marks found in her secret parts." Webster pleaded not guilty, and on June 1, 1863, she was acquitted. At some point after the trial, Philip Smith, a church deacon who had been a member of the court that had considered Webster's case in Northampton, said he had tried to help her because she was poor, but she said something to him in reply that made him fear she might try to harm him. Smith then became ill. To the people who attended him, there were some strange things that happened during his sickness, as reported by Cotton Mather in *Memorable Providences*, a book published in Boston in 1689, excerpts from which are included in *Witch-Hunting in Seventeenth-Century New England*. There was a musk-like smell, the source of which could not be identified; there was a scratching sound near his feet, and sometimes fire was seen on the bed. Something as big as a cat was observed moving under the covers, but when the covers were lifted, nothing was found. These and other occurrences made people think that witchcraft was at work. Smith died of his illness. Mather was convinced that Smith had been murdered by witchcraft. While Smith was still alive, some local men, convinced of Webster's guilt, decided to take the law into their own hands. This is the description given by Sylvester Judd in *History of Hadley, Including the Early History of Hatfield, South Hadley, Amherst, and Granby:*

Compare & Contrast

- **Late 17th century:** The Salem witch trials begin in Salem, Massachusetts, in June 1692. Many people are denounced as witches as a wave of hysteria sweeps across the town. Within three months, nineteen men and women are convicted and hanged. Another man is pressed to death by large stones for refusing to submit to a trial.

  1990s: The Salem Witch Museum in Salem, Massachusetts, which opened in 1972, uses the three hundredth anniversary of the trials to bring a sense of reconciliation and an understanding of the lessons to be learned from them. In 1991, Pulitzer Prize-winning playwright Arthur

Miller (author of the 1953 play *The Crucible* about the Salem witch trials) is the featured speaker at the opening press conference. In 1992, the museum helps to form the Salem Witch Trials Tercentenary Committee and oversees the building of the Salem Witch Trials Memorial, adjacent to Salem's seventeenth-century Charter Street Burying Point. Nobel Laureate and Holocaust survivor Elie Wiesel visits Salem to dedicate the Salem Witch Trials Memorial.

Today: The Salem Award for Human Rights and Social Justice is given each year to keep alive the lessons to be learned from the witch trials of 1692. The award recognizes those who work to end discrimination and promote tolerance. In 2013, the Salem Award is given to Thomas Doyle, an ordained priest, who helped to expose sex abuse within the Catholic Church, and Horace Seldon, a former minister of the United Church of Christ, who has spent forty-five years teaching about racism and working to end it.

- **Late 17th century:** In Europe and North America, witchcraft is considered evil, a deviation from true religion, and witches are persecuted.

1990s: Wicca, a pagan religion developed in the early twentieth century in England, combines witchcraft with other beliefs and rituals. In 1990, Wicca has 8,000 adherents in the United States and is popularized in films and television programs, such as Charmed, a TV series aired on the WB beginning in 1998, about four witches who practice their art for good rather than evil. Popular books such as The Truth about Witchcraft Today (1998) by Scott Cunningham, disseminate knowledge about Wicca and witchcraft.

Today: Wicca is a fast-growing religion, with 342,000 people identifying as Wiccans in a 2008 survey. Wiccans venerate nature and are forbidden to harm anyone. Many practice their beliefs alone, not connected to any organization. The status of Wicca as a religion has been upheld by US court rulings.

- **Late 17th century:** Estimates of the number of alleged witches killed between 1484 and 1700 in Europe range between 200,000 and 300,000. **1990s:** Witch hunts no longer take place in North America or Europe, but they continue in other parts of the world. The BBC reports that, in the Democratic Republic of Congo in the late 1990s, children are being labeled as witches. People in Congo society are superstitious, and when misfortunes occur, many blame them on sorcery committed by children. More than 14,000 accused children in the capital city, Kinshasa, have been thrown out of their homes onto the street. Others have been murdered by their own relatives. The BBC also reports on the murder of alleged witches in Tanzania.

Today: Persecution of people accused of being witches still continues in Africa, India, and other parts of Asia. In February 2013, in Papua New Guinea, a twenty-year-old woman is accused of sorcery by relatives of a six-year-old boy who died in the hospital. The woman is tortured and burnt to death on a pile of tires and trash, watched by hundreds of people.

A number of brisk lads tried an experiment upon the old woman. Having dragged her out of her house, they hung her up until she was near dead, let her down, rolled her sometime in the snow, and at last buried her in it, and there left her; but it happened that she survived.

Mary Webster died in 1696, at about the age of seventy.

Critical Overview

Although Atwood's poetry has not attracted as much critical comment as her novels, "Half-hanged Mary" has received some attention from reviewers and literary critics. The reviewer for *Publishers Weekly* includes "Half-hanged Mary" as an example of "the most vivid poems" in *Morning in the Burning House*, which "forge an apprehensible human aspect from scholarly fields of science, history and religion." In her review of *Morning in the Burning House* in the *Antioch Review*, Molly Bendall comments, "Atwood's savage, back-talking dramatic monologues have become her trademark," including "the tour de force 'Half-Hanged Mary,' a voice from the bleak theatre (Salem chapter) of our history." For Ray Olson, reviewing the same collection in *Booklist*, "if she [Atwood] is not consistently persuasive, she is always vital, powerful, magnetically readable." For Kathryn Van Spanckeren, in her essay "Humanizing the Fox: Atwood's Poetic Tricksters and *Morning in the Burned House*," "Half-hanged Mary" "recalls *The Journals of Susannah Moodie* [another poetry collection by Atwood] in its chronological construction and transformation from realistic woman protagonist to mythical figure (in this case a witch). It evokes a consciousness mysteriously continuing after death." However, Van Spanckeren adds that "after all her suffering Mary remains emotionally dead and cut off from others."

What Do I Read Next?

- *The Handmaid's Tale* (1985) is one of Atwood's most famous novels. It takes place in a dystopia in the near future and explores the dangers of totalitarianism, religious fanaticism, and the devaluing of women. The United States has become the Republic of Gilead, a conservative Protestant theocracy in which women are strictly controlled in all areas of their lives. The novel is narrated by Offred, who serves as a Handmaid to the Commander, a powerful member of the government. Her only role is to produce his children.

- Atwood's *Selected Poems II: Poems Selected and New; 1976–1986* (2nd edition, 1987) contains seventy-three poems, including selections from four of her previous collections as well as seventeen previously unpublished poems.

- *The Door* (2007) is Atwood's first collection of poetry since *Morning in the Burned House* in 1995. These fifty poems explore topics such as writing and the role of the poet, time, aging, and mortality, as well as political and environmental themes, including war.

- Carol F. Karlsen's *The Devil in the Shape of a Woman: Witchcraft in Colonial New England* (1998) is a history of witchcraft in New England from 1620 to 1725. Karlsen examines gender relations during the period and argues that alleged witches were primarily older, sometimes financially independent women who were perceived as a threat to the dominance of men in society.

- *Teen Witch: Wicca for a New Generation* (1998) by Silver RavenWolf is an introduction to Wicca for young people. The author, at the time of writing, was the mother of two teenage children, and she understood the concerns of teens. She explains the basics of the Wiccan religion and takes a practical approach to spells and rituals. She emphasizes that magic does not mix well with alcohol or drugs and that Wiccans do not harm other people.

- Like Atwood, Alice Walker has major achievements in both novels and poetry. *Absolute Trust in the Goodness of the Earth: New Poems* (2003) is her sixth collection of poems. The title conveys one of the themes of the eighty-six poems in the collection. Walker employs simple diction and mostly very short lines as she writes in praise of the beauty of life in all its aspects and offers thoughtful reflection on a range of emotions.

Sources

Abrams, M. H., *A Glossary of Literary Terms*, 4th ed., Holt, Rinehart and Winston, 1981, p. 45.

Atwood, Margaret, "Half-hanged Mary," in *Morning in the Burned House*, Houghton Mifflin, 1995, p. 58–69.

Bendall, Molly, Review of *Morning in the Burned House*, in *Antioch Review*, Vol. 54, No. 2, Spring 1996, p. 248.

Demos, John Putnam, *Entertaining Satan: Witchcraft and the Culture of Early New England*, Oxford University Press, 2004, pp. 3–15, 63, 81–82.

Evans, Ruth, "Eyewitness: Suspected Witches Murdered in Tanzania," BBC website, July 5, 1999, http://news.bbc.co.uk/2/hi/africa/386550.stm (accessed February 22, 2013).

Goldman, Russell, "Real Witches Practice Samhain: Wicca on the Rise in U.S.," ABC News website, October 30, 2009, http://abcnews.go.com/WN/real-witches-practice-samhain-wicca-rise-us/story?id=8957950 (accessed February 22, 2013).

Hall, David D., ed. *Witch-Hunting in Seventeenth-Century New England: A Documentary History, 1638–1692*, Northeastern University Press, 1991, pp. 7, 261.

Judd, Sylvester, *History of Hadley, Including the Early History of Hatfield, South Hadley, Amherst, and Granby, Massachusetts*, Metcalf, 1863, p. 239.

Linder, Douglas O., "The Witchcraft Trials in Salem: A Commentary," Salem Witchcraft Trials 1692 website, September 9, 2009, http://law2.umkc.edu/faculty/projects/ftrials/salem/S (accessed February 22, 2013).

"Margaret Atwood: Biography," Margaret Atwood website, http://margaretatwood.ca/bio.php (accessed March 5, 2013).

"The Official King James Bible Online," King James Bible Online website, http://www.kingjamesbibleonline.org/Exodus-22-18/ (accessed March 5, 2013).

Olson, Ray, Review of *Morning in the Burned House*, in *Booklist*, Vol. 92, No. 1, September 1, 1995, p. 32.

Review of *Morning in the Burning [sic] House*, in *Publishers Weekly*, Vol. 242, No. 35, August 28, 1995, p. 107.

"The Salem Witch Museum – Past and Present," Salem, MA: Salem Witch Museum website, August 2010,
http://www.salemwitchmuseum.com/media/SalemW (accessed February 22, 2013).

"The Salem Witch Museum – Timeline," Salem Witch Museum website, August 2010, http://www.salemwitchmuseum.com/media/timeline (accessed February 22, 2013).

Shumaker, Wayne, *The Occult Sciences in the Renaissance: A Study in Intellectual Passions*,

University of California Press, 1972, p. 61.

"Spectral Evidence," Salem Witch Museum website, February 13, 2013, http://www.salemwitchmuseum.com/blog/ (accessed February 23, 2013).

Tatlow, Didi Kirsten, "Women Killed as 'Witches,' in Papua New Guinea, in 2013," in *International Herald Tribune*, February 19, 2013, http://rendezvous.blogs.nytimes.com/2013/02/19/wo tortured-killed-as-witches-in-papua-new-guinea-in-2013/ (accessedFebruary19,2013).

"2013 Salem Award Winners Announced," Salem Awards Foundation website, 2013, http://www.salemaward.org/ (accessed February 22, 2013).

Van Spanckeren, Kathryn, "Humanizing the Fox: Atwood's Poetic Tricksters and *Morning in the Burned House*," in *Margaret Atwood's Textual Assassinations: Recent Poetry and Fiction*, edited by Sharon Rose Wilson, Ohio State University, 2003, pp. 107–108.

Vine, Jeremy, "Congo Witch-Hunt's Child Victims," BBC website, December 22, 1999, http://news.bbc.co.uk/2/hi/africa/575178.stm (accessed February 19, 2013).

Further Reading

Cooke, Nathalie, *Margaret Atwood: A Biography*, ECW Press, 1998.

> This is the first biography of Atwood. Cooke explores the ups and downs of Atwood's private life and her emergence as a major figure in Canadian literature and culture.

Howells, Coral Ann, *Margaret Atwood*, 2nd ed., Palgrave Macmillan, 2005.

> This introduction to Atwood covers her work from the 1970s up through the novel *Oryx and Crake*, published in 2003. Howell explores all of Atwood's typical concerns, including Canadian identity and feminist issues.

Howells, Coral Ann, ed., *The Cambridge Companion to Margaret Atwood*, Cambridge University Press, 2006.

> This is an examination of Atwood's work in all genres. The introduction traces trends in Atwood criticism since the 1970s, and the twelve essays by Atwood scholars analyze her work from a variety of critical

standpoints.

Stein, Karen F., *Margaret Atwood Revisited*, Twayne Publishers, 1999.

> This is an introduction to Atwood's major literary works that discusses theme and character, as well as her storytelling style and frequent use of paradoxes.

Suggested Search Terms

Margaret Atwood

Half-hanged Mary

Mary Webster AND witch

witches

witchcraft

witchcraft AND New England

Salem witch trials

dramatic monologue

Wicca

Ingram Content Group UK Ltd.
Milton Keynes UK
UKHW021946080523
421401UK00015B/1040